In Sleep's Circumference

In Sleep's Circumference

— POEMS

Charles Sabukewicz

Published by

For Helen, always

We are such stuff as dreams are made on,
and our little life is rounded with a sleep.

— The Tempest

CONTENTS

The Land Of Plenty

Twilight —

Dreamer's Pillow

A cloud, a halo, a sail blown full—
conveyance to the weightless edge
of crossing over
with softened face
and breath barely a whisper
by a dream compelled
beyond parentheses of time
outbound toward Polaris
the lighthouse blazing there
safe harbor just beyond.

Out of the wind's murmur
a gale rises
tears loose the sail
blasts my ship
with the thunder-shock
of a reef-torn hull
the mast splintered
the dark angel calling
my body swept away
in a riptide of stars—
only to awaken
adrift in the pillow's down
concerned about the time.

THE LAND OF PLENTY

A Carousel Rider

It was a fractured constellation,
all glass, glitter, calliope blasting,
an engine with whirring belts
and giant ponies lunging up and down
shuddering on golden poles.

The pony my father sat me on
was red-tongued, its jaw taking the bit,
eyes wild in flight. Given to that pony
against my will, cut off from the earth,
I rode screaming at the pony's rush.

In dizzy, reckless orbit,
whipped forward lunge after lunge,
a red-faced bawling boy, a pony
with a wind-stunned forelock
and a wild indifferent heart.

Fighter Pilot

I eased my Thunderbolt
down for a desktop landing
where I penciled it in—
a hieroglyph of war,
its guns hot from battle
a shell hole in the star insignia.
Wiggling a loose front tooth with my tongue,
I opened the canopy and tumbled out
to do my arithmetic.

Geography was next.
I traced Columbus' voyage
in a deepening pencil groove.
My tooth's blood tasted good
a tiny fountain leaking red
sent up from my slow volcanic heart
its thug thug thug
keeping time with the pendulum clock
and oh my aching itching feet
wanting to run, to tumble me
into a pigpile at recess
a joyous burial, dark smothering fun
in coats, leggings and snotty cuffs.

My tooth broke free
a tiny agate grinding against the others.
Calling on me, my teacher asked,
What was Columbus searching for?

Marbles

The special ones
I held to the light at home
smoky colors woven in glass
imaginary planets to touch, rub
make hot in my hands
their histories known by heart.

A sweet fever— the lovely greed
in bagging the captured ones,
nestling them in a cloth bag
my mother made for me.

My best was the heavy duty killer
in my hip pocket
a big boy slugger
translucent blue
last to risk
in the random dirt of the schoolyard.

The Land of Plenty

God loved our worn out shoes
clothes we had to keep for best
our hair wet down and parted
glazed faces we wore in church.

We loved the dirt we played in
jack knives and pointed sticks
wax teeth at the candy store
holy medal good luck charms.

We learned about the afterlife,
a "forever" after this, but luck
and fingers-crossed held our
confidence. And what if sin

put black marks on our souls?
We knew that lies and bb guns
had the greater gravity. Girls
caught our attention and soon

were undressing in our minds.
Nothing, it occurred to us, was
as it seemed to be. One day we
awoke to exile, happy to be free.

Slip-ons

They had wrinkles where they bent
and dark holes he slid his feet into.
My father kept them lined up
on the floor beneath his suit.
They had tabs for pulling them on
and a gold buckle on the side.

Big oceans for me,
they flopped about, cool
and leathery smooth. The wrinkles
looked like waves, gentle ones,
depending on his mood,
sometimes a hurricane.

My shoes—all scuffs and scars.
His had special powers, making
him tall at the altar rail
delivering the Sunday offering,
dark and mean sometimes
for no reason I could tell.

He'd polish them,
rubbing the dark paste in,
buffing them with a rag,
bringing them to a shine,
the best he had to offer,
his one good pair.

Motorcycle

Oh, bright ghost of my father
riding the skylit fires
of a two stroke engine,
wearing a mask of ice
on a subzero night,
riding to the war factory
forever in my mind,
racing down Route 1,
the rage of the engine
propelling you through time,
ice rimming your goggles,
subzero air
ruffling your knit cap.

You rumble past
the airfield on the coast
where fighter planes take off
practicing night runs,
the gunners hunched
in their chilly cocoons,
the pilots reading the stars.

You are a ghost now.
It is near midnight,
and you ride bent low in the cold,
your knees locked on the metal frame,
your eyes fixed on the road.

Archaeological

My father in chaos
gone without warning
his atoms lost
to graveyard dust.

His faint reflection
in my mirror
casts light enough
to find my way.

Watch, work boots
tiny gold filling
pocket full of change
remembered artifacts.

I saw him in a dream
a house painter
home from work
coveralls flecked

with rainbow colors
visor cap askew.
I sift these sediments
in time's hard clay

that my dream of him
not decompose, that I
recall his smile, that
the past is not a grave.

Small Town

When we were growing up
nicknames were the hard currency
we willingly exchanged,
tags sticky enough to last a lifetime
body blows for some
or hard jabs resonating day after day
like target practice for those
skilled in the art.
Jughead, Mouse, Ratman.
Choirboy, Beaver Tail.
Born in fun or the delight in torment
they were poison arrows
wounds meant, some parents said,
to get you ready for the real world.
Some kids fought back.
Some didn't.
You had to be tough.

Calendar Girls 1952

Standing by the tool bench in Hade's Garage, I pretended to watch
the mechanic fine-tune a carburetor until its rough idle turned soft
and satisfying and he dug his blackened fingers into a can of white
goop, slicking up the grease on them just enough to come off easily
in the deplorable towel anchored in his back pocket so he could
break for coffee and a donut, but my eyes kept switching to the girl
on the calendar—holy mother of God her breasts tore open the veil
of innocence, everything The Legion of Decency warned about
without naming of parts and believe me this truly was the radiator
of my blood overheating because I'd been wondering lately about
the red hair of the girl three rows over in history class and now I was
Satan's partner and it felt good and maybe I should give equal time
to her eyes and rosebud smile and not be totally greedy regardless
of whether I was guilty or if just to look was a venial or mortal sin.

And then, nosed up against the window of the defunct timekeeper's
shed at the abandoned railroad station, I stared into the shadows
on its back wall where the calendar girl sitting on the edge of a bed
in the painful cold of late afternoon had been waiting for her lonely
voyeur so addicted to her dark hair and the sweet revelation of her
breasts, an insatiable novitiate in that desperate, flat world of pretend,
living in exile beyond the dusty pane, the weathered window frame,
the thin, dead air padlocked in shadowy space, day, month, year so
imperceptible I could only imagine what it would be like to tumble
into the Eden of her breasts, a sweet promise of utter delight
in the blue cold of that room and the hoped-for world to come.

Black Lightning

Freeze cracks howled that night on the lake
when I skated away
from fire-lit voices on the shore
out and out and out until
the planet and I were all alone.

Urged by the blunt cold
the weight of ice worked against itself.
Near and far its tension
like cracked glass
sang whip-like into the woods.

I sped on a frozen circle
felt stars on my skin
heard their silver sound
rode their light
fled before their wind.

A Shipping Clerk

Even when I shouted, the weavers
had to bend close to read my lips.
It was hot.
Sprinklers overhead misted the air
so the rayon wouldn't stick.
Shuttles sped back and forth in loud slaps,
each strike like a sharp base hit
multiplied by a hundred looms
churning out rolls of striped cloth
to become linings for raincoats and jackets,
thick spools of color feeding hammering shuttles
in a wilderness of noise.
We hung our lunch buckets
from long strings attached to the high ceiling
to make it harder for the cockroaches.
The money was good.

ECG

Many years I've lived
with a whisper in my blood,
a cloudy, troubling hiss
in the knocking in my chest.

Awaiting sleep I'd listen
to my heart repeat "I am"
with heroic imperfection,
a lisp in a scarred valve.

Now tired beyond measure
each heartbeat's urgent flash
records in stark upheavals
and rumbling aftershocks

a dark, voltaic mountain
whose rugged tracery
hides chasms and fault lines
beyond which none can see.

A Wake-up Call

At 5:00 am God looked into my casket
and asked, "Why aren't you asleep?"
"Because I can't," I said. "I've been awake
for hours. And what about you?"
"I never sleep," He said.

The Two Next Door

The floors had squeaked for years,
dry wood complaining that the nails
could no longer hold them steady,
an SOS to the living space above—
where music was and water dripping
in the sink, the kitchen timer now
and then, the jangly phone, laughter
in the living room. Back and forth
and in and out the two of them: she
who so loved her gardens he would
say, "The earth loves your hands."
And she in return: "The stars have
given you your poems." In spring
there were forget-me-nots, peonies,
a bleeding heart. Her aconites were
his favorite, a grace note at the end
of winter, impervious to the morning
frost and the wind bullying the trees.
Why does he dream of things so far
away? she wondered when she read
his poem about Andromeda, recalling
the dragonfly she shared her garden
with one summer morning long ago.
Sometimes they spoke of loved ones
lost and the hardships of growing old.
As long as she had her gardens and
he his stars, it seemed their faded rugs,

rain gutters stuffed with leaves, and
furnace troubles now and then were
of no concern amid their busy lives.
They were convinced their portion
was the best eternity could offer.

Self-Storage

The snow saddens to a sunless gray this afternoon
as I sit here looking out over the street
and thinking how time has unraveled my best sweater
how all our closets are full
and there's no place to put anything
except maybe rental space in one of those low, windowless
rectangular buildings north of town
a phalanx of concrete storerooms for the ashes of our daily
     lives:
bureaus, bed frames, photo albums, hats and shoes,
leftovers for safekeeping behind pull down doors,
each unit a dark cubby hole
in the pyramid of an afterlife
where we try to hold onto something
we may someday need.

Upon his Eyebrows

The ropes and pulleys of their musculature
allow the man behind the curtain
to glide from doubt and worry
to joy or arch superiority
or even scorn if need be, not that I
would ever call upon the latter two.

He's an artful actor in my employ
whose job it is
to provide a variety of masks:
convivial self, deep thinker,
rogue, playboy, beast of love,
or fallen angel looking
for the best way back.

And what now that the once blond arches
so long expressive of an endearing self,
have been roughed up by gravity
into a white shrubbery
indifferent to the casual snipping off
of those in full rebellion? A warning,
perhaps, that I can no longer play
a scoundrel by Moliere? Not that I would.

This rascal, scamp, knave
would trample on my lines,
emote a leer, a jibe, so willingly unkind.
Am I his master or is he mine?

In Meditation

I am seated here in my darkened room.
I'm also in the back yard
changing the lawn mower's spark plug.
Now I'm remembering the dental floss
I forgot to buy. I sit up taller, trying
to look and feel dignified. I breathe
softly, engaging my familiar mantra:
"In with the new, out with the old. In with…"
It is April. The lawn is nicely green
and our ancient red oak ever so slightly
begins to suggest that the annual February
death notice I assign it is again premature.
Tiny buds it has. Stingy and glacial
in their slow and stubborn report.
My mind is wired to a gravity of unrest.
Thoughts shamble in with their baggage
of tired monologues and worn-out ideas,
unwelcome guests dumping themselves down,
happy to be home in a seedy hotel.
Shirley Bassey is belting out Goldfinger.
It's as if my mind is worried about itself,
and trying to solve all my problems
by throwing in a lot of clutter
to plug the hole of silence that might break in.
I linger in the pause between breaths.
Each as it comes is a limpid pool
within a circle of grasses and reeds.

I sit in its shelter. I am at peace with my body.
I rest without effort. I am empty. And then,
like a spy without country or cause,
I slip through a narrow door
and poke my head into the universe.

At the Clock Repair Shop

Their insides exposed, their cogs and gears,
springs and pendulums
sprawled at every angle everywhere
on work benches, counters, window sills:
useless hands on silent faces, so much time
stopped, spilled out: grandfathers
with dead chimes, wooden trays
thick with pins and screws and weights,
time time time
stripped for parts to be used and reused,
decades of love, death, and happiness
dispersed into the void.

And now, apprehensive, in awe of the chaos
in this corner shop above the village waterfall,
we tender into the owner's hands
a family heirloom, our ninety year old
mantle clock, its numerals
useless behind the window glass
of its wooden shell.

Examining our clock's condition,
he shares with us his love of the trombone,
his weekend gigs, the tempo of his life.
We scan once more the ruins all about,
failed machines overrun by time,
catastrophe he's comfortable within.

With fingers crossed, my wife and I
step out to the street,
thinking about the pendulum's restless sway
we count on, even when lost in sleep.

The Stone Cat

Outside our window, the stone cat waits
in meditative pose, tail tucked aside its belly,
eyes gazing at us as the falling snow
erases her silhouette and the stone bench
she rests upon until she vanishes as if
her spirit leapt away to cross the white lawn
and disappear into the trees, leaving us
our memories of the cat who once lived,
often quick to come home when we rang
a little brass bell, its thin, tiny ring singing
into the woods to call her from the hunt,
her secret life, a black dart suddenly racing
from somewhere in the high grass, the bushes,
the many trees, sometimes to make an offering
of a mouse or vole, or gifting us with a burr,
but time caught up with her: a white whisker,
then aching hips, a long search for comfort
in lying down, in sleep draping herself
over my wife's hip; awake, curling in my lap
like a part time muse. In remembrance one day
I stepped out to ring the bell and felt her spirit
come to me, a final gift from the dream edge
of an unknowable truth we know is true.

Tadasana

I have learned over time
the map of my body,
its scars, fault lines,
a continent
imperceptibly adrift
in some greater plan
to reunite itself
with the rib work of the earth.

An old cartographer,
I map the best I can.

Standing in our pond,
head erect
toes spread
in muddy sediment
I rest awhile
in the pose of the mountain.

Of the Mountain's Calm Desiring

I look to the mountain east of my window,
a slumped silhouette, its contours
worn away by a glacier long ago.

It is a gruff old mountain, an old hump
indifferent to the weight of time
in the dark of its substrata:
four hundred million years
meaningless, except that they
are something I am measured by.
I understand my brevity.

Stone with roots of stone
anchored to upheaval
forests as they first appeared
fire scars and rocky creeks
a cloud cap in the sun—
a cycle of birth and death
and earth's regeneration.

THE HOUSE
OF METAPHOR

In Motion, Poetry

Into the little tributary of the mailbox
go my poems
to enter a stream of poems
from all over America,
sonnets, tercets, free verse
seeping into post offices
mail trucks, cargo planes,
a continental sea of poems,
the best
bobbing up and down amid
the green, the overripe—
tons of flotsam and jetsam
at the edge of which, editors,
like beachcombers on sunlit islands,
wade into the undertow
looking for gold pieces
and bits of colored glass.

The Secret Lives of Poems

Until you arrive they live like shut-ins
waiting in darkness. They are bored
with their room mates
and obsessed with occasional gossip
whispered through the paper-thin walls.
Otherwise, they have little to think about
but their personal histories
which they mine again and again
often with great pride, keen memories
of the lighted world and sometimes
fame, or even notoriety.
According to the grapevine,
some of the newcomers among them
are quite snotty, one of whom they've heard
has a nose ring and frightening tattoos.
She's restive, hungry to see daylight
as they all are
but indifferent to the old timers
one of whom is two thousand years old.
Of course, beyond reminiscences,
there is little genuine discourse here
except for the tired debate between
rhyme and free verse. It gets ugly sometimes.
None are shy. However, over all,
they are not an open book.
Perhaps you can pry something out of them.
If you visit, remember:

they like attention of any kind. Find the right key
and say them so they can hear themselves.
Even if you only read them silently
they feel your presence.
Stay awhile. They shine when read aloud.
It reminds them of when they were born.

Surface Tension

From the well of a half-full coffee mug
I draw what inferences I can
to explain the sad chaos of my notebook
where I've been looking for a few good lines.

My pages are littered with half starts,
none of which wants to assume a life of its own,
a thread of words spilling out of my ball point
hot-wired to go long distance and take me with it.

My coffee is tired and so am I.
I can taste the burn in it
like the burn I can feel in myself.
I am waiting for something on the periphery,
perhaps some weight-bearing words
laden with charged particles of time,
then a line or two maybe breaking into a poem
with some light-bearing words slow to decay,
a narrative to be shaped in a rhythm of *just is*,
lines that compose a little house of metaphor
held in place by my breath.

A Resurrection Man

After too much time working in the graveyard
of unfinished poems, where midnight ground
is littered with broken metaphors and cracked
headstones, where disappointment's weather
has blurred the lettering of reluctant epitaphs,

I with sorrowful laptop take one last long look.
Over here lies the hunter with the wooden leg.
Here, a beautiful woman forever imprisoned
in a beginner's charcoal sketch. Here, ten lines
about angels doing time in an umbrella factory.

Such promise at the beginning. So much hope.
Such wild attempts to resuscitate early drafts
with prayer, cheap merlot, workshop séances,
so much verbal compost wasted on the rose
and a sonnet twelve years now on life support.

*It is madness to think such plinth and shards
could one day be whole again*, said my muse,
phoning me from her office in the silver dawn.
Still, the earth here is sweet familiar ground
seeded with fragments that yearn for the sun.

Bone Dry

Lately I've been unable to dream.
My muse is somewhere in New Mexico tonight
sleeping with a cowboy under the stars.
Unfaithful muse,
so quick to live in the body of another,
she who once clung to me
leaving notes under my pillow
teasing me with a telepathic swarm
of words and images I'd often use
to sing how beautiful she was in sleep:
dark, tangled hair
inviting smile
feminine parts in wonderful display.
She will not have it so tonight.
Say something, lover boy.
"You say something," I reply, feigning confidence.
realizing from the tone of her voice
she wants my resignation.
 "Give me something to work with,"
I whisper into the night.
Even now her warm, magnetic field
is screwing up my watch.
"Look. I don't mind you having been with
Milton or Shakespeare or the others or …whomever,
but…a cowboy?"
 I've rediscovered rhyme.
"I'll bet you have."
Besides, you're no Milton
or Shakespeare. Get some sleep.
I'll send a line or two in the morning.

Inferno

Dead to the world I dreamt
the flames of metaphor
were menacing a wind-up clock
alarmed that I was running out of time.
My room was ablaze with metaphors
igniting the sofa, ravaging the walls.
Sparks of implied comparisons
settled on books and magazines
and nestled in my beard.
"Fire!" yelled my poems, their fingers
scraping the lid of a cardboard box.
"Get us out of here. Fire!"
"I melt!" wailed the candle poem.
"Air!" cried a poem about northern lights.
"I need air."
"How fitting," said a free verse Halloween mask.
"I knew it would end like this."
In a jagged haze I grabbed them
and made my way to the fire escape
where I set them free, watched them
flutter into starlight as they whispered "goodbye"
until, in a fit of panic, I winged after them
gathering them one by one
in my fingertips.

A Baggage Claim

His pen carries a cargo
of unused copies of his signature
ready at a moment's notice
to touch down on a clear runway
and release his identity as a poet
who might have something to say
but hides his ego in his luggage
along with dozens of rejection slips
and the names of people
nobody knew he loved.
There he is on the white tarmac
wondering if anyone is waiting for him
and trying to decide which way to go
hoping for a taxi to a modest hotel
where, with an easy confidence,
he'll sign the register
as if there were an auditorium nearby
crowded with poetry lovers
dying for him to appear.

An Ego Trip

After the poetry reading,
the brandy, the self-congratulation,
Mr. Provo Profundo retires to bed
with an ego the size of an observation balloon
and soon enough
he is hoisted into the night
in a basket loaded with a kayak,
boxing gloves and bags of incendiaries
to drop on enemy lines
firing at his ship with their artillery,
the pop pop pop of their flack exploding
with the sound of pulled wine corks
their shrapnel
peppering him with free verse.
One by one he lights the fuses of his poems
and casts them over the side:
starbursts of couplets
and rondels cracking open
lighting the faces of the lesser poets
their tin helmets strapped to their chins
their grim faces
troubled by the whole idea of flight.

An Angel in my Closet did Appear

All clocks in Paradise move backwards,
she whispers through the louvers. She's
busy among my shirts and ties, digging
through my sport coats' pockets, even
trying on my shoes. It's three days now.
When I ask her to come out, she refuses.

She smells like ink and parchment, emits
a soft, flickering, summer lightning glow
though it's winter and the days are short.
She whispers in dialogue as if rehearsing
testimony: polishing, reshaping, arguing
on behalf of some hapless soul near lost.

I ask her what kind of trouble she is in
and to stop playing with those matches.
She flexes her stormy, iridescent wings.
Behold, a ray of sunlight is my sword.
My banner is a hummingbird's wing.
I tell her I'm a poet. Maybe I can help.

I slide a new sestina through the louvers.
A cloud is an anvil, she cries. *Beware.*
Justice shall smite like wings of a moth!
That's my poem on fire! My neckties!
She's using my coat to snuff out flames.
A cardinal matter, I'll call the authorities.

Trouble With Commas

Littered with the tiny hooks
dangling from the back edges
of words the river of thought
slows to a meandering stream
loaded with a sediment that
erodes the riverbanks of nouns
drags down the big fish verbs
rests finally in the dead zone
of grammatical correctness.

Entering the current of the
sentence, cast a line long
and loose, let its thread spin
easy the bait of thought
until, in the quick-fire strike,
you feel through the hook
the muscular heart, the fine
bone of metaphor caught
in the art of the moment.

A Grammarian's Lament

Some considered me a tyrant
snapping the red whip of a cross-out
or a savage underline to make a point
along with my calm insistence
that it should not happen again.
But it did. Even a draft dripping red
couldn't stop the flood of transgressions.
Sensitivity is all I asked, quiet consideration
for those final touches that grace good writing.
Crack the whip I did.
I importuned, ranted, bickered
drummed drummed drummed it in
until, like one of Poe's characters endlessly pacing
in the gloom of his ruined castle,
I lamented the lost beauty
of proper usage and gave up the ghost.
Now the barbarians run amok: the period,
once a stout guardian at the intersection of ideas,
no longer a match for speeding run-on sentences;
the shapely comma, its soft femininity,
once a discrete stay against confusion,
now promiscuously applied like an easy woman
ruinously spreading her charms; the semicolon,
hermaphroditic, wanting to claim authority,
but unsure of its identity; the colon,
hating its name, insisting it be addressed
as "cologne" after the French and bitterly tired
of being used for grocery lists and weekend to do's.
These were ever my pretty ones, who,

like eternals in the universe of composition,
brought reason and order to a chaotic world.
And I, made irrelevant by cultural *laissez faire*,
have retired to the peaceable kingdom
of reading the classics
with their elegant sentences marching by.

An Element of Style

A noun by definition
can be almost anything:
an ounce, a bone, a tempest, a tiger,
but by itself
a noun sits helpless on the page:
the ounce feeling weightless
and unimportant,
the bone, though hard, durable
and proud of its history,
can't even lift a finger.
The tempest, well,
you can imagine the wind and rain
of its destructive power
totally one-dimensional.
And then the tiger
majestic in stealth and ferocity
forced to lie in wait until
a verb comes along, any verb,
tug, or push or pull or snarl
so it can pad over to sniff the ounce
or lick the bone as a trophy
of its last conquest
or dig its fangs into the tempest
because it isn't afraid of anything,
neither man nor gun,
the deadliest nouns of all.

String Theory

Thank you for the poems
and the hand-written note attached.
The characters of your signature
look like children holding hands at recess
just daring me to run at them.

I've often thought that a name is no more than
pieces of string curved and looped
into someone we think we are.
Tied together and pulled tight, it becomes
a fill-in-the-blank where our identity goes
or a time line of our chronology up to this moment
or a black thread that a spinner's hand
runs through the eye of a magic needle
to make enough space for us to live in.

I can see by the flourish of your last name
it's become a weathered house
with an attic full of coloring books
and nursery rhymes, stories about animals,
and in the basement perhaps
a walled-in memory of the moment you first learned
that rejection is like a handful of wasps
and an antiquated form like the sonnet
might not be the best vehicle to undo the hard knot
of the mystical entanglement
of being alive. Thank you for submitting.
We hope you find a place for your work.

The Prisoner of Art

The artist in the Cathedral of the Blind
longs for his freedom. Day after day
he rubs dream fingers across his memory
of stained glass windows, their leaded ribs,
the Braille of robes, halos, and upturned eyes,
the anchor, the crown, the lamb,
wings strong as lightning bolts.
He would escape from this darkness
and the flutter of his heart,
his only hope to bring forth an angel
from the tip of a #2 pencil, a miraculous angel
relevant to the age of quantum physics,
of space finite and infinite, an angel
created from memory, one robed only
in pencil shades of gray on white,
an angel that might free him
now suddenly appearing
only to find herself shaken
by the beauty of color surrounding her,
stained glass so vivid she longs to be bedecked
in red, the color of the wounded saint,
longs for a golden halo, longs for wings
in the colors of the rose window, wondering
at the logic of her pale essence whilst
her powers exceed even those of the archangels.
What have you done? she asks the terrified artist.
Give me eyesight and I shall tell you, he replies.
You please me not, she says bitterly. Look at me.
And he sees, and is pleased with the work of his hand.

A Poet's Christmas Carol

It is cold out here on Water Street.
Snow leaks through the cracks in my shoes.
My cuffs are threadbare, so is my skull.
Winter has no end.

I turn up my coat collar. Poetry is hard.

I want buttons ablaze with celestial fires,
my words ringed with St. Elmo's light.
My collar and necktie should glow and shine
like a coin from an angel's pocket.

In fingers crouched like a thief,
the pen spins thin, blue threads
to rob quicksilver images
and make them indelibly read,
only to slip away:
the butterfly you may not touch
or ruin its powdery wings.

The work of a lonely angel,
regard the poet shuffling by,
one part in the stars,
the artful libertine of words,
composing in drowsy tones
his only real estate,
the wind's imperial blast
down a midnight street like this.

Snip one bright button from his coat.
He'll find his way by the stars.

Exile

Determined to make progress
in his notebooks, the young poet,
after hounding his children into quiet,
is shipwrecked at his desk.
A steam radiator
nudges him toward sleep.
His wife has slipped into a novel.

On his island reef
of pens, erasers, and broken pencils
he prays for lost sailors
and keeps watch in hopes of rescue
while at low tide
fragments of unfinished poems
dabble at the shore.

THE NATURE OF THINGS

The Woodpile

Trees we have burned
in rough chunks split into wedges
burned them
in round, hardwood loaves
dry, combustible, hotly singing.

Maple, birch, oak
have been taken,
the chain saw's teeth
blazing through rings of time
a shrill razor tearing the air
with the hot roar of combustion
a kind of fury
an emblem of extinction
howling in the woods.

The cut lengths dry in August air.
Their seasoning cracks open
to the fire they will become.

Thermodynamics

At zero degrees outside
I fill the kettle
set it on the burner
and dial HI.

Warmth, I'm told,
has too much space to fill
and cold
has ample room to kill

When the kettle howls
I scald the cup full
watch the tea bag whip its tail
pull in the tag
and bleed the darkening dye
of energy coming to rest.

Even if all matter
is doomed to come
to a cold equilibrium,
time is delicious.
I sweeten it
with a spoonful of honey
dropped into the warmth.

Some Say in Ice

One spider hid in the bathtub all day.
Another crept from behind the mirror
to see if the light was out.
Cold puffed in at every seam of the old house.
Angry, ruler-thin streams clouded the dismal rooms.
Floorboards shivered; the furnace barked obscenities
and the thermostat sighed.

He watched in desperation
as the TV spilled a weather report
into the room. Cold. It rumbled
up his legs till he crabbed on his knees
over a matchstick flame.

Winter struck like a white hammer.
His girlfriend wouldn't answer the phone.
The pipes froze.
His avocado turned to stained glass;
the jade died in its sleep.

When the final frost settled steel blue
on cupboard and floor,
the sun flared out like a shattered headlight
and he slipped into the loving arms
of the goddess Hypothermia.

The Blue Woodstove

It is a rugged engine
hungry for oxygen,
primitive
with restless exhalations,
a steady pulse
of seething, rippling heat
spun
from its cast iron crucible.

It is a microscopic star
armed in blue significance,
feeding now
as its trim flames sing
in the molten bones
of its turbulent wood.

The window glass reveals
catastrophe within,
the stormy transmutation
of wood and oxygen,
a mystery of trees consumed,
their passages
through sun and rain
transformed
to strident golden flames
by ancient gods
who whisper
the language of the cosmos.

A Brief Liaison

Lunar Eclipse
February 2, 2008

Tired of living as the sun's reflection
tired of his attitude as master of the house
knowing when he's done with her
he will take away his light,
she slips into a thin red dress
a rosy cloud in which
her body opens to this earthy one
wanting him to take his time
give her the raw sweetness she likes best
when, under the door, a knife edge of light,
footsteps on the stairs and—no time
to say goodbye, no time for anything
but to hide her dress, compose herself,
wait for the crush of his blinding light.

Cabin Fever, March 15

Tonight's temperature will drop into the 20's.
Light snow is forecast.

The red-winged blackbirds
have arrived in my notebook.
They'd been looking for my sketch
of some telephone poles
and the pond down the road.
They flew in behind a pencil line
tracing the bulge
of an imaginary warm front
moving up from Virginia and Massachusetts
and now all over this page
blackbirds are swaying atop cattails
perching on power lines
fluttering among the reeds
their loud *checks, tee-errs* and *honk-la-rees*
signaling the others to come in
and settle here
until the weather improves.

Orion in Spring

The old giant
retreats to the west
belt blinking
limbs
melting in twilight.

Of what use now
his glimmering shield,
his powerful arm
wound tight
to send the fatal blow?

April steals
his patch of sky.
Time for him to leave.
Even his dog
nips at his heels.

Courtship

Emily in her dream chair is aroused by the sun
rubbing up against the clapboards of her house,
teasing the veil of moisture beneath their paint
just enough to lift some color off, working on
the little round hats of nails to draw them ever
so slowly out, even now working on her arms,
her breasts, finding a surprising warmth below,
and who in the neighborhood would know about
this April transient, a handsome roustabout leaning
against the alcove's windowpanes, showing off
his magnetic gaze as if she'd die to be in his arms,
follow him down the road as he warms flowerbeds
and stirs up clouds of bees, finding it impossible
to keep up as he hurries past the cemetery, erasing
shadows as he goes, beckoning her to come, lie
down with him, take refuge in his hot white light.

Summer Crossing

An incidental toad
beside the garden stone,
caught by my arrival
in the speckled sun,

awaits my move
to strike or amble by
uses its camouflage
to elude an enemy

and risks a fatal blow
indifferent to chance,
a prehistoric choice
for such amphibians.

Instinctively it hops
beyond my fingertips,
bumps across the lawn,
down the garden steps

to await another eon
behind hooded eyes
under sheltering ferns
and apocalyptic skies.

The Swallows at Coles Pond

If their flight could be remembered
as imaginary threads suspended in air,
delicate lines
of blue or green or gold
mapping each glide or arc,
lines bold and taut
or whimsical and wild,
lines weaving in and out
of the bird box in our yard,
rainbow trajectories
filling the air beyond our porch
with prisms of color;
if their flight, in all its creative mystery
could be held articulate in our memory
long after the swallows have gone,
after summer has ended
and frost stiffens the ground,
would we then radiate
the light of our reverie to those around us?
Would we become messengers of light,
sewing with our words and gestures
a lyrical quilt
wherein our stories are told
in the beautiful threads of the swallows flight?

Solar

Little that is new
can be said about the sun:
the day's eye
the hero of our story
light that warms the face
and heart, light
steady in its burning, quick
to arouse a field of crops
or slow to nurse a pot of seedlings
on a window sill
a pagan god on the beach
in the melt of a summer afternoon
a roughneck
with fists of wind and tide
and a lover
holding us in thrall
feeding our spirits
forcing us now and then
to cover our heads
as a sign of respect.

A Wave Rider

This is our time in the sun
the dangerous season of bodily form
exposed to the heat of a star.

Drowsy radiation pours over us like jazz
warmth so delirious that bathers masquerade
in brilliant fabrics, sunglasses and oils.

We hide in parachutes of shade
or step into the sea while camera minds
turn like weathervanes. We try to be discreet
but observation is impossible unless we look
and all eyes look when Leah crosses the sand
in her bathing suit's pink light.

She dips her painted toes into the water's edge,
strides out in easy equilibrium to slip beneath a wave
and turns to await the next one gathering speed.

Arms outstretched, she times the curl to catch just right
the lip of collapsing surf. Tons of sea skid, drag,
pound their way toward the sandy beach,
wrapping her shoulders in a white scarf,
bearing her landward in an arrow of white spray.

Line Storm at Watch Hill

Low pressure stuns the barometer.
The sea's armistice is blurred and torn. Flags explode.
The lighthouse goes out in a roaring black cloud.
Squalls of gray and white hiss at windowpanes.
Thunder rips the air. In the wind's temple,
towers of ocean and weeds, sand and stones,
batter, roar, shred the storm charts,
broil through the broken afternoon.

Tomorrow, tourists will come to hike the dunes
and photograph the placid waves, the gutted beach.
The mansion on the path to the lighthouse will dry in the sun,
its caretaker scowling at the torn awnings
and ravaged window boxes.
From my window I'll watch some riders top the hill,
athletic as their bikes pour down the shiny street.
A decent storm, I'll think,
as sunlight leans across a page of my journal.
Beyond the jetty, a fishing trawler from Galilee
will curve south into a light breeze.

Heraclitus at the Compost Bin

Harry feeds his garden elemental rot
from a paradigm in a black vat,
vinyl, sun-warmed, its cookery a flux
of egg shells, oak leaves, melon guts,
sugary bruises thickened to a stew
turned with a spade over slow summer days—
an earth bread, a medicine, a black, home brew.

Firebugs

A twist of the ignition key
slaps the motor awake
sets in motion
illusions of transcendence
over space, time and matter
on the way to the mall
to buy a slug of satisfaction
for an endless, aching need.

Muffled pyrotechnics
under the shining hood
allow us to get SOMEWHERE
all weather-proofed
air-conditioned
sheltered from the sun
because we can
because we are busy gods
using what we've learned from lightning
to flick light switches
and set the thermostat,
to nestle thermonuclear heat
into rocket cones,
to melt our glaciers
with the keypads of computers.

At the Landfill

A dead bulldozer rusts
in a patch of goldenrod.
The landscape is littered
with mattresses, bed springs,
orange peels and blown-out TV sets.
There's old man Whitman
picking through the junk.
He looks skeptical.

All this blue, burning energy has cooled
to a strange coagulation of parts.
Sea gulls, with cries like winches
and rusty pumps, wait nervously
on their beach of discarded tires.

The horizon is a collapsing universe,
an iconography of power.
The fallout slows, hardens.

Islands of ragweed pollen
flare and balloon into the atmosphere.
August is on fire.

Nothing but Stars

They are loved in their spheres
loved in their endless progression
somewhere through time,
loved in their luminosity
their spectral incandescence,
faithful in their velocities,
proud, divergent, significant of destiny,
stunning us in our imagination of their heat,
dangerous to our minds, pulling us
into the seas of their dark landscape
into endless emptiness unimaginable
where we are lost and insignificant
but lighting our way, telling us of themselves,
wanting names, named by the ancients,
masters of themselves, their fragments
their seething rays;
the stars, our creators, created us
to tell about them
to whisper their strange distances
to love them to their last red embers
to the black tomb
wherein they too must someday depart,
their colors bleached to blackness
to the zero of absolute.

The God of Lost Cats

By death's quick edit to delete
from moonlight's silver narrative
our cat's nocturnal drift, a moon
full and thick, a moon so brazen
it blinded the scattered stars even
as it stamped an imprint of sharp
edged shadows on the lawn,
traced hedge and tree, mapping
the way to the best kingdom ever
of mouse and vole, describing in
summer's deceptive Braille thrills
of the hunt, the midnight feast,
luring our large gray cat to stray
into woods deep and shadowless
and cruel beyond our sleep's safe
circumference and our certainty of
his usual safe return, dream lulled,
while he, embraced in the moon's
gravity, wandered as the moon did,
and, without trace of blood drops,
without shrill keening of the fight,
took with him the sad history we
long ago had rescued him from, red
tattoos of scratches, broken tooth,
bitten ear, shedding the rough habits
of homelessness, establishing his
own identity, rescuing us from our
busy ways, and now vanished, not
by aging's slow abbreviation, but

by some hidden illness, or by guile
of fox or coyote, or by the stealth
of some sullen god of lost cats, his
sweet and sturdy bones forever lost
in the woods, his time with us now
a gray and silver narrative we repeat
as we drift into fragmentary dreams
we hope to somehow find him in.

TWILIGHT

The Wild Rose

How quick and surprising
the bright spark of pain
at the finger joint
where the thorn enters,
a tiny injection blossoming
into a purple bruise,
the moment laden
with ancient texts:
the tree, the serpent, death—
the shiny point of the thorn
inviting fear into the mind,
not of this momentary wound,
but of the darkly playful universe
waiting to call us back.

Insomnia

O for a pinch of sleep
a nubbin
a penny's worth
a veil dropped down
on the waking world
to carry me under the sea
my arms full of ocean
in the dream light of stars
their colors flashing
on sea-pounded cliffs
my breath echoing
in a rhythm so easy
I doze till the moon
floats up like a silver button
and slumber
comes in on the tide.

After Dark

That bed we attend by night—
that seedbed of dreams
where we ease into the shell of sleep—
that storybook garden
nourished by the mind's eye
with symbols and meanings
often hidden from ourselves,
all conjoined into colorful narratives
of improbability and utter truth:
weightless but falling helplessly
or caught in a divine paralysis
in a place of no return we return from,
often to forget the marvelous stories
we would otherwise die to tell,
or sometimes haunted by fears
we are tongue-less to relate—
that is the bed in which we play such parts
as lovers or clowns or demons,
a dark stage under a canopy of stars
where roam wolves and bats and bears,
whatever our sleep's imagination
conjures up—that is the place
we tend like groundling gardeners
who revel in the stuff of dreams,
yet never hold the key
by which we enter or leave.

Course Correction

Trying to figure my position
in relation to the stars
silver graphics spread across immensities—
the hunter, the shepherd, the bear
travelling together as if they know the way
but drifting apart, their story an illusion
borne on celestial turbulence
while here in my living room
amid billions of galaxies
on an odyssey of my own
with star charts strewn before me,
philosophies, theories, holy texts,
I plant my oar
on the stormy coast of the cosmic narrative.

Be an Angel, Will You?

No. You are not ready for astral projection.
Wings are for beginners. Wings.
It's a tradition here. Try these.
Slow, but they'll get you there.
Of course the feathers and straps
are vulnerable to cosmic winds
and star-burn you wouldn't believe.
You'll get used to it. All travel is by night.
You must learn to avoid black holes.
We don't use a compass.
Just plot the shortest distance,
usually a straight line, but not always.
Look, here on the celestial planisphere.
You've been called to a nursing home
near Alpha Centauri, right?
The 94 year old woman in a wheel chair?
The one who asked her caregiver to be an angel?
Follow this line. This is the route you take.
Sometimes space bends or wobbles.
If your rigging detaches, you've got big trouble.
Memorize the address.
Buckle up. That's it. Make it tight.
When you get there, take her out to the patio.
Tell her she is beautiful, that her wheelchair
is a chariot, that its spokes flash like jewels
in the morning light.

At the Umbrella Factory

The seamstresses are Angels with delicate hands.
Lightly go the treadles of their machines.
Lightly go the supervisors pacing the aisles.

On the hour, inspectors test the working parts.
Visitors crowd in to see umbrellas open and close
in rhythmic bursts of color.

In the rainbow room, Apostles work
on scenes from Breughel and Degas.
Seraphim embroider lines from Emily Dickinson
on funeral umbrellas.

Having just visited the Reliquary,
tourists watch, fascinated, wondering
if it actually rains in Heaven,
and should they buy an umbrella
just in case.

The Mousetrap

It is a door latch to lightning,
a spring compressed on a thin board
and cocked like a gun.

Red quarter-moon of apple,
the smoke of decay
burning into the night.

In a bed as cold as the Atlantic,
the astronomer enters sleep,
his bedcovers rumpled
like a white-lipped wave.

He dreams of tiny teeth
about to unhook
the brassy sway of planets,
a fireworks for the little brain,
a red stripe for a thief.

Within the hour it comes,
searching the universe
for a lost crumb.

Drummond and the Blue Ashtray

Even his jacket smells of smoke
like a sleazy cloud
hiding him from himself.
He senses victory
destroying himself like this
closing in on the mystery of God
measuring his lack of faith
against the cosmic scale
whole tempests of hydrogen clouds
and moody suns out there.
There is always death
the way cigarettes are dead
in the blue ashtray
stiffs in broken jackets
jabbed extinct.
He feels like that sometimes.
He resurrects a butt
and scratching a match on his shoe
lights it.
With a long, unhealthy drag
he blows the smoke upstairs,
feeling like a god
lit up by a penny sparkler
a face amid the clouds.

Captivity

Upon the shot glass hour
the bottle in his drawer
sleeps snugged up nicely
with his socks, underwear,
and life insurance policy.

His bottle is a bully god
magnanimous and sullen,
a dark hour companion,
in proof a living spirit
redolent with bronze fire.

Free now seven days,
he dreads his boozy self,
that hurly burly predator
with razor beak and claws
whose narrative unfolds

like a reel of horror film:
a pinch, a tumbler,
a harmless friend at first,
until his speech turns sly,
then claustrophobic jeer,

sagging lips and eyes,
a ruinous, zigzag world.
The thug in the bottle
shakes his slumber off,
wings spread full.

Ishmael's Dream

They come ashore by night
heavy men in oilskins
and black boots
rough men from the sea
bringing the wind's howl
the thundering surf
blunt talkers
searching my books
letters, scribbled notes
casting my nautical maps
into the fire.

Their wind-raw faces
are dark as woodcuts
their beards black
scrawly, rain-wet
their thick hands
thumbing page after page
looking for something
I do not have.
A lightning flash.
A ship's bell sounds.
I move with them
out into the storm.

Metropolis c. 2095

It's a dark business
working in the print mine
late at night, newspapers
stacked miles deep,
tons of print
compressed beyond belief,
bylines, obituaries,
catastrophes, comics
pulverized
under the stupendous weight
of their existence
until they leak into
a river of black, a chaos
of feeding tubes, bullet wounds,
hat tricks, underwear,
no end
to the nightmare sludge.

Here's an article
about the pound of spiders
you will eat before you die
and... there it goes, down
with the rest,
heartbreak and high hopes
ever so slowly moldering
into a rich, black compost,
stuff they pay good money for
to put on farmers' fields
in a galaxy
where the only story is entitled
A sweetness without name.

At the Space Terminus

Weightless in deceleration
ideas glide into their docks
and lock in place.
Pilots loosen their helmets,
tired after six billion miles
of philosophical discourse
some without sleep
for ten thousand years
thinking how even brotherhood
grows tiresome
and cargoes of paintings
novels and mathematical formulas
only go so far in relieving
the emptiness of space.

They know the old routine
of Welcome Home!
the space platform brightly lit
doctors   lawyers arsonists and angels
waving flags, laughing in anticipation.

Here we go again, mutters one pilot
a geopolitical specialist longing still
to see the snow he'd read about
and wondering if rain speckles a pond
before a thunderstorm
(read in a poem near Andromeda)
and wondering how big a bite
Eve took from the apple

and were her breasts
like pears in the still-life he'd stolen
a million years ago
and hidden in his luggage.

Beautiful Dreamers

Death is a temporary champion
a cosmic nibbler
who would eat your heart out
and spirit you away, saying
in the rhythm of your heartbeat
good boy, good boy,
all the while dropping clues:
the socks lying on the floor by your bed
like starveling has-beens
or letting gravity do the job
or filling your mind with static
when you try to penetrate the awful silence
that positions the moon
as a stony reminder of what fate is.
But these are fleeting moments
in the cosmic scheme of things.
The truth is your atoms are here to stay,
to become a leaf, a raindrop, a grain of sand.
So, tell death you're not going anywhere
and when by night you leave your other self
and slip into your dreams
you add another chapter
to a fantastical autobiography
light years in the making.

Parallel You

If it is true, as I've heard theorized,
the universe recreates itself
every millionth micro-second
so seamlessly you wouldn't notice,
a constant process of stop and start,
I can only wonder what happens
during that blip in space time
when everything—your sweater,
socks, knees and ankles, nose,
even the room you're sitting in
or the rear-view mirror
you casually put your trust in
while doing 85 on I 95
vanishes.

Could time transport you
into another story, another fate
that saves you from the collision
that was in the plan, or the phone
that didn't ring when it was supposed to,
or that sketchy heartbeat
totally ready to quit,
and off you went in a continuation
of the life you expected to happen
seamlessly melded into a parallel
universe, in which no one even notices
your arrival, the other self left to die
or be divorced or win the lottery?

Supernova

This current, this starry flood,
this river
of numbers, theorems,
this musical mass
of time, distance, light,
this swirl
of starbursts, hydrogen clouds,
of atoms and molecules,
of weather, mountains,
this ancient rushing river
of starscape, planet,
this moment
of creation, destruction,
this churn of light rising,
blasting foundation stones,
seeping under doors,
into cupboards, cellars,
light tearing at sills and trusses,
trickling into
lockets, photo albums,
images
of mother and child,
playground, park,
light swelling, rushing
its locomotive thrust
swallowing phone,
watch dial, wedding ring,
cloud reflection, poem,
this burgeoning tide
flooding, gathering

thorn, crucifix, graveyard dust,
lightning bolt and bee
all all all
swept up,
flooding, deepening,
the long tide rolling,
thundering, a sea now
boiling in the churn
of triangle, parallelogram,
the chop and chuff
of numbers
in black magnitudes
88888888888
crashing
in sea foam, scud,
sign, cosign, formulas,
decimals broken,
light-sodden pages,
the last light now
a thin line on the horizon
as the wind rises and voices
call in the dark
a bedlam
of words
echoing in the shrouds,
the taut skin of the sail,
words
throated, lipped,
words words words
spilling
in catastrophic rush
into the windy darkness
the void

April Homily

Praise to the songbird found
in the gloom of an organ pipe
here at St. Stephen's. Praise
for this creature long interred
in the fluted wind, the flutter
of pedals and stops, the chortle
and thug of full-throated pipes,
their history long aglow with
birth, death and resurrection.
Praise to the parable of life,
the winged narrative by which
a songbird fell un-witnessed
into the dark, its found bones
wrapped in a shroud of decay,
entombed in the music of joy
and sorrow, to take once more
this day the sweet imagined air
of that morning's open doors,
a wild creature in panic flight
lost in the stained glass hues
of the lamb and the crown,
circling above the heads of the
devout, rushing back and forth
through a flood of prayer, the
lyric exhalations of the choir,
the offering, the peace, suddenly
and miraculously to disappear.
This April morning, years after
its long fall into silence, let it

remind us of those long missing
from their pews, at home in the
Kingdom of star and planet, of
light years, hydrogen clouds:
space time's miracle unfolding.

Stargazer

Mornings she would check the weather
notate any dreams she could recall
and with coffee at hand set to work on an old typewriter.
She loved the certainty in the sharp click of its keys, the way
it chiseled her words in graveyard black.
In its tattering voice she found the words she needed
as if the machine were a medium, a doorway to Zodiacal light.

Her work done by noon, it was out to the mailbox
to cast her words into the tidal flow of print
where the lonely, the hopeful, the lost, ordinary people like herself
might find in her daily column advice to navigate a world
of wrong turns and tragic moments.

As a child she'd learned to love the midnight gleam of planets,
having been told by her mother the stars were hers to tend,
a silver garden handed down by the ancients
who believed the stars' cold radiance was laden with destiny,
silver threads to sort and glean and read
according to the moods of their various constellations.

She and her mother had lived in old house near Breadloaf Mountain
where the night skies brought them closer to the stars.
At the edge of sleep she would imagine
the rugged wheel of the heavens turning,
its iron rim of stars in flight grinding out their narrative:
the ram, the scorpion, the archer, the crab, the fishes,
the solar clock marking the ecliptic:
filaments of starlight to be untangled,

their dark netting once entered
sometimes offering no way out.

In high school, she had tried to be invisible.
She was a quiet girl left to her own powers of observation.
One day in morning study hall she reluctantly passed along
a scribbled note. Another followed. Then another.
It seemed she could be trusted, but secretly opening some of them
she found scribbled warnings, crude anatomical sketches, gossip,
misspelled words and words sadly beautiful.

Boys were a madness to some girls
but not to her. She'd take her time.
She felt the stars had made her cold and bright,
that they had a plan for her.

Late at night she wrote love poems at the kitchen table,
dreamed herself into a top-down red convertible,
her headscarf wild in the speeding wind, her ringed fingers
in the lap of the wild boy in dark sunglasses
who sullenly sat next to her in study hall.
She dreamt she was the fastest girl and the cops were after them.
She understood that the moon could hurt.

"Like cheap jewelry the stuff you write,"
her husband said the day he walked out.
She was standing over the sink and staring out the kitchen window.
"What do you know about fate?" he asked. "Look at us.
What's your friend the moon got to say about us?
If you're so wise, how come you didn't see this coming?"
She wanted to say she knew, but couldn't find the words.

How lovingly strange her mother had been.
She'd wanted a child but not a husband.
She chose the man and had the child,
a girl who would never know her father.
So mother and daughter had lived in various places,
moving and moving again, until one day, as her mother told her,
"This is the place. Our place. The sky is beautiful here
and the winters are cold. Here we'll stay."
The house she continued to live in was her mother's legacy,
as were the stars, her closest companion.

It was the shock of the expected actually happening.
She never thought he would do it, her craftsman husband,
a hard man with delicate hands and the love of wood,
a close reader of oak and maple and cherry,
their grains, their knots, their soft curves.
He was as quiet as the hills around their home,
a good and sturdy man, capable of beautiful work,
but moody and brooding, boiling underneath.

And now she lived alone.
Her mother came to her in dreams at times,
a mother who had a poet's heart,
a woman who mistrusted men,
a strong woman even to the end
when her days were running out.

Now there was little else to do but live in the calm of knowing
the stars had their plan. Even in her darkest moods,
her undercurrents of doubts, she took strength in the self-knowledge
of being ordinary but kind, believing against all reason
that the stars entwined her into their being,

that their legends were true, that their light
was her mother's greatest gift to her.

What else was there to love except the hills around her,
her vegetable garden, her flowers, her restless dreams,
the drive down the mountain road to the town below?
And years of writing her horoscopes, caring confections
she sent out into the world. Did they snare any cynics?
Were they publicly scorned but privately peeked at, just in case?
She had heard it said that we are made of stardust,
atoms to atoms and dust to dust. After all, the night sky is a city of light,
so many stars brightly colored in reds and blues and greens,
flickering their way through the Zodiac while the planets glow
and the faithful moon watches over her silver provinces.
The sky is a perfect garden really, a busy seed bed, a place of final rest.

CPSIA information can be obtained at www.ICGtesting.com
Printed in the USA
BVOW06s0528160416

443477BV00012B/29/P